PORTFOLIO STRUCTURING AND THE VALUE OF FORECASTING

Jacques Lussier, PhD, CFA, Editor

CFA Institute
Research
Foundation

Statement of Purpose

The CFA Institute Research Foundation is a not-for-profit organization established to promote the development and dissemination of relevant research for investment practitioners worldwide.

ISBN 978-1-944960-08-7

August 2016

CONTENTS

CE Qualified Activity CFA Institute

This publication qualifies for 0.5 CE credits under the guidelines of the CFA Institute Continuing Education Program.

Foreword

On 8 October 2015, CFA Montréal hosted its annual Asset Allocation Forum under the theme "Portfolio Structuring and the Value of Forecasting." Two asset management approaches were compared:

- The factor investing approach, which relies on identifying common factors in security returns, determining which factors represent compensated risks, and then extracting returns from a larger and more balanced set of compensated risks than traditional cap-weighted indices do

- The traditional approach, which relies on explicit forecasts of security—or industry-specific expected returns made by asset managers

Traditional asset management has sustained much criticism in recent years. Few active managers outperform their benchmark after fees over longer time horizons, such as 5 to 10 years. There has been much empirical evidence supporting the view that professional forecasters cannot predict or that their predictions explain only a very small part of the variability of asset returns. Hence, many investors are starting to embrace factor investing, which is becoming more commoditized and is often accessible at a lower cost.

However, even the factor investing approach relies on forecasts of expected returns, although the forecasts are implicit. Factor investors are not forecasting that the utility sector is likely to outperform the energy sector by X% over the next year (an explicit forecast), but they make the implicit forecast that, for example, value stocks are likely to outperform growth stocks in the long run. Hence, both approaches rely on some form of forecasting.

The objective of this forum was to shed some light on the factor investing approach, often called "smart beta," while discussing recent developments in forecasting capabilities that may spur renewed interest in traditional asset management approaches.

The conference attracted five top speakers in their respective field. Two of these speakers discussed the factor approach—Andrew Ang of BlackRock and Mark Carhart, CFA, of Kepos Capital. The other three speakers discussed our ability to predict—Craig Bodenstab, CFA, of Orbis, David Rapach of Saint Louis University, and Philip E. Tetlock of the University of Pennsylvania. Each speaker wrote up the most important aspects of his speech, and the write-ups are included in this brief.

ON FACTOR INVESTING

Andrew Ang literally wrote the book on factor investing (*Asset Management—A Systematic Approach to Factor Investing*). In his write-up, Ang explains factor investing in a highly intuitive way. He describes the types of factors that exist (macro and style factors), the rationale for the existence of such compensated factors, and the ability to deliver factor products. He also explains that the factor approach can be used to easily and efficiently demystify the performance drivers and risk exposure of the most complex portfolios. The factor approach can become a powerful way of running an entire asset management firm.

Mark Carhart distinguishes among factors (he uses the term "exotic betas") as sources of risk premiums, uncorrelated returns, and opportunities captured by unique management skills. He proposes a taxonomy for the classification of factors and insists on the need for a strict set of criteria to properly distinguish a true factor from a spurious correlation. He also makes the argument that, although building portfolios with equal exposures to the various risk premiums is a reasonable starting point, there is value in varying the factor exposures over time either because of structural changes or because it may be possible to make reasonable correlation forecasts. He then uses a conservative simulation that incorporates transaction costs and significant performance haircuts to illustrate the potential of such an approach.

ON FORECASTING

Craig Bodenstab adopts a realistic view of forecasting. In scientific disciplines, knowledge is cumulative and built on strong foundations; in finance, knowledge is greatly influenced by our own experiences. We continue forecasting despite our horrendous track record because "I don't know" is not an answer that investors appreciate from their managers. Moreover, even in situations where we can correctly predict (such as, under certain circumstances, GDP growth or the tremendous growth of the information technology industry), Bodenstab demonstrates that this valid information does not always translate into accurate asset price forecasts. Hence, in his opinion, investors should put more emphasis on what they do control—how much they are paying for an asset.

On the other hand, in recent years, we have made significant improvement in the accuracy of certain kinds of forecasts. Phil Tetlock published a landmark book in 2005 called *Expert Political Judgment—How Good Is It? How Can We Know?* Tetlock tracked the less-than-stellar forecasts of 284 experts over two decades. His work triggered the launch of a four-year forecasting tournament sponsored by the

US government's Intelligence Advanced Research Projects Activity (IARPA). The project run by Tetlock was done under the auspices of the Good Judgment Project. It won the tournament by a wide margin. Steve Rieber, the program manager at IARPA, summarized the results as "the largest improvement in judgmental forecasting accuracy observed in the literature."

Tetlock shows that it is possible to make better forecasts of certain phenomena but that better forecasters must have the right mix of traits. They must also limit themselves to forecasting things that are forecastable—trying to forecast tomorrow's closing value of the Dow Jones Industrial Average, for example, is a bad idea. Furthermore, forecasters can become even better when properly trained in probabilities and bias awareness. Continuous feedback and keeping score on good and bad forecasts is also essential to the learning process of forecasters. Tetlock's work is documented in his recent book written with Dan Gardner, *Superforecasting—The Art and Science of Prediction.*

Finally, David Rapach reminds us that forecasters face substantial model uncertainty and instability when forecasting asset returns, which present keen challenges to practitioners. However, significant progress has recently been made for improving asset return forecasts despite those challenges. He presents two approaches that significantly improve forecasting efficiency and warrant the attention of investors.

Each of these five researchers makes a distinctive contribution to our understanding of the asset management framework. Perhaps the next breakthrough will be the integration of efficient explicit forecasts with factor-based approaches.

Jacques Lussier, CFA
CFA Montréal

1. Factor Investing: More than Simply Investing in Factors

Andrew Ang, PhD
Head of Factor-Based Strategies, BlackRock, Author of *Asset Management: A Systematic Approach to Factor Investing*

INTRODUCTION

Factor investing strategies systematically hold non-market capitalization weights of securities with an aim to harvest broad, persistent drivers of returns. Investors taking on factor risks have the potential to be rewarded in the long run with return premiums in excess of broad market benchmarks.

The foundation for factor investing is the belief that a parsimonious set of these return drivers—called *factors*—determine the long-term expected returns of all securities across and within asset classes. It is helpful to think about factors to investments as nutrients are to food. Both milk and steak contain fat and protein—just as public equities, private equities, high-yield bonds, and most hedge funds are exposed to economic growth. Eating a healthy diet requires looking through food labels to their underlying nutrients. Just as an athlete training for a marathon requires a different mix of nutrients than someone recovering from a chronic illness, different investors have different optimal factor portfolios. **Figure 1.1** illustrates this metaphor.

Factors come in two types: macro factors and style factors. The effects of macro factors, like inflation and economic growth, are most clearly seen across asset classes: High inflation is bad for both equities and bonds, for example. Styles of investing, like value—searching for cheap securities relative to their intrinsic worth —are also factors because we observe style premiums within and across asset classes: sovereign bonds, global credit, developed and emerging equities, commodities and currencies, and even private markets like real estate.

Factor investing directly targets these broad, persistent drivers of returns via strategies designed to hold optimal combinations of these factors based on investor needs and to implement them in an efficient, low-cost manner. Many now use the term "smart beta" to describe those factor portfolios that are long-only and done within

FIGURE 1.1. NUTRITION FACTORS AND INVESTING FACTORS

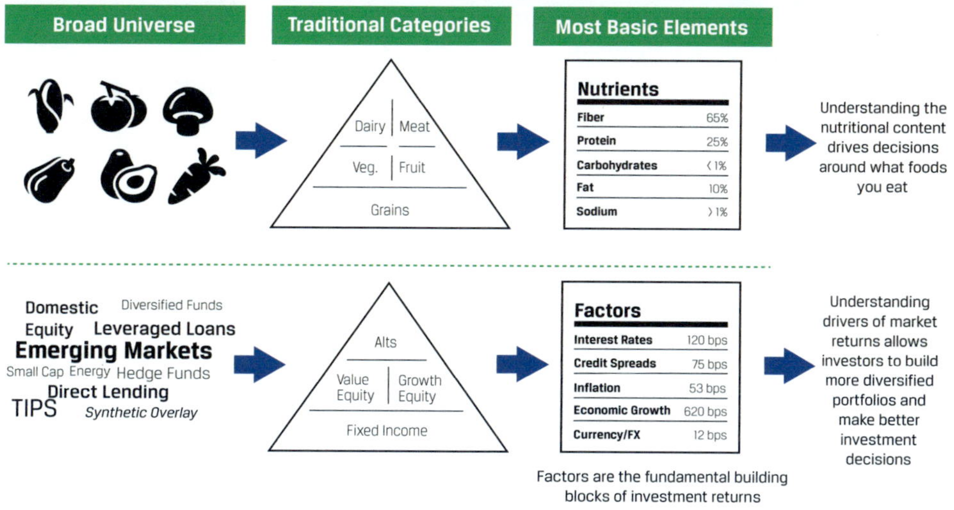

an asset class. Smart beta is a benchmark-driven form of factor investing. But, factor strategies can work well, and there may be even better investment opportunities available than just equities, when implemented in long–short implementations across multiple asset classes.

Importantly, all of these factor premiums—and the methodology for implementing these factor premiums—are well known. The academic theory that there are multiple factors driving investment returns dates from the 1970s. Professors have also demonstrated that macro and style risk premiums have been exhibited in centuries of data.[1] What is new is that data, technology, and new investment vehicles have made factor investing affordable and scalable in a way that was not available even just a decade ago: New investment techniques have *democratized* access to factor premiums, but the concepts behind factor investing are old.

With one exception: the recent institutional focus on factor investing has brought to the fore one area that is truly new to the practice of asset management. And with this development, the most innovative factor investors have transformed their whole enterprises.

[1]BlackRock, "Smart Beta: Defining the Opportunities and Solutions" (2015).

GROWING POPULARITY OF FACTOR INVESTING

Interest in factor investing has grown tremendously dating back to my advisory work for the Norwegian sovereign wealth fund in 2009. Many asset classes performed poorly during the financial crisis over 2008 and 2009. Many asset owners with traditional asset allocation frameworks did not anticipate these losses; simply allocating to "hedge funds" or "private equity" did not provide effective diversification because many funds in these asset classes were exposed to the same factors as those driving bond and equity markets. Factor investing looks through these asset class "labels" to focus on the underlying drivers of returns.

Since 2009, the investment environment has been challenging. At the time of writing in 2016, nominal bond yields are negative in several countries, and short-term rates in the United States are still hovering close to zero. Equity markets remain on the expensive side, as measured by long-term price-to-earnings and other valuation ratios.[2] Factor investing concentrates on those factors expected to have long-term rewards and seeks to minimize exposures to unrewarded idiosyncratic risk. In doing so, it seeks to improve risk–return trade-offs. Some factors are under-represented in investors' portfolios; the converse is that their portfolios often skew to only one or two factors: economic growth as was apparent during the financial crisis,[3] for example, in their total portfolio, or momentum in a portfolio of external managed funds. Holding a more balanced mix of factors can improve investors' risk–return trade-offs.

The majority of institutions have not given up on alpha—the ability to generate returns in excess of factors—but they are more wary and want to elucidate the actual value-add generated by active managers. Factor strategies are relatively cheap. Factor strategies can often be complements to, and in some cases replacements for, traditional active management. In particular, enhanced factor strategies that can harvest factor premiums in multi-asset, long–short formats can be good complements to hedge funds. In an era where every penny counts, asset owners want to ensure their managers are delivering performance that cannot be passively replicated by low-cost factor strategies, and factor analysis can illuminate those managers delivering true alpha.

[2]BlackRock, "Smart Beta."
[3]BlackRock, "Smart Beta."

WHERE DO THESE MULTIPLE FACTOR PREMIUMS COME FROM?

If the largest institutions are practicing factor investing and the theory and empirical evidence behind factor investing has been known for decades, then the natural question is why do these premiums continue to persist? What's the economic basis behind these factor premiums?

There are three reasons why factor risk premiums have endured for many decades despite being well known:

Reward for bearing risk. Investors may be compensated in the long run by a risk premium for the potential losses produced by factor strategies during bad times.

Structural impediments. Certain constraints, like leverage or regulations driving certain types of institutions to some preferred types of securities, may give rise to style premiums.

Behavioral biases. The preferences of average investors may cause them to overvalue certain securities and ignore others.

MACRO FACTORS ARE REWARDS FOR BEARING RISK

The "big three" macro factors are real rates, inflation, and growth. Investors exposed to these factors can experience losses when real rates suddenly spike, inflation is high, or growth is anemic. (Other important macro factors include credit, emerging markets, and illiquidity.) These often define "bad times" in the short run. In the long run, an investor may be rewarded for holding assets that benefit from "good times": periods of low or decreasing real rates, low and steady inflation, and high economic growth. The rewards in good times may outweigh the losses in bad times, so in the long run, there may be a factor risk premium.

Macro factors largely determine the returns of overall asset classes. Macro factors are broad: Equities largely reflect economic growth risk, but there is also an important inflation and real rate component of equity returns. Economic growth also manifests in other asset classes. Macro factors are also persistently rewarded: The rewards for growth were studied in security markets by the earliest classical economists in the 1800s, and the ravaging effects of inflation were felt even in ancient empires.[4]

[4]William N. Goetzmann and K. Geert Rouwenhorst, *The Origins of Value: The Financial Innovations that Created Modern Capital Markets* (London: Oxford University Press, 2005).

STYLE FACTORS MAY EXIST FOR REASONS OTHER THAN REWARDS FOR BEARING RISK

When we say that equities reflect growth risk, we are making a statement that the average stock—which we generally proxy by a market capitalization-weighted index—is exposed to growth. There is, at any moment in time, a dispersion of stocks around that average. Long investment experience and a large body of academic research have found predictable patterns in the dispersion of stocks that point to return premiums. These are style factors: value beats growth, winners beat losers, low-volatility stocks have higher risk-adjusted returns than high-volatility stocks, and quality outperforms junk. Style factors drive the dispersion of stocks within an asset class, whereas macro factors drive asset class levels of returns. **Figure 1.2** illustrates these concepts.

FIGURE 1.2. FACTORS, RETURNS, AND ASSET CLASSES

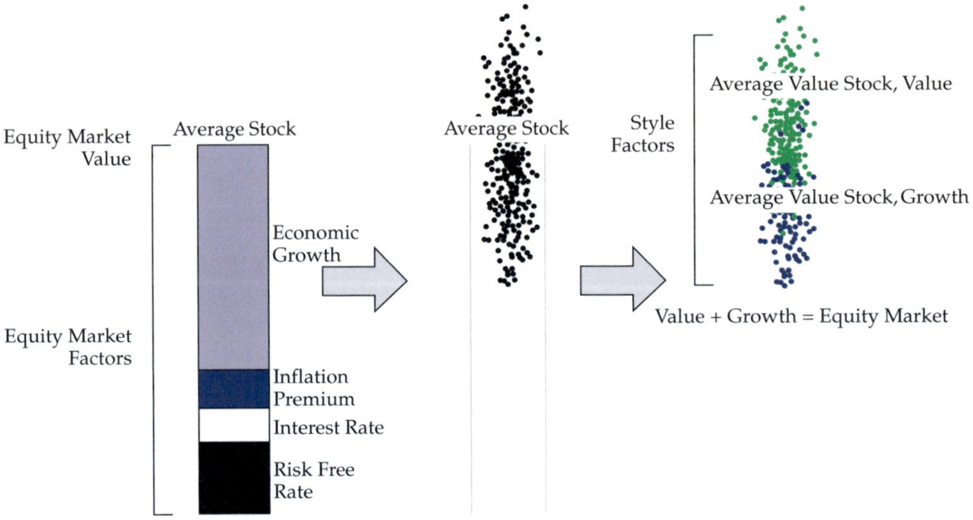

Note: For illustrative purposes only.

One notable difference between macro and style factors is that the style factors take on just one side of the market; the macro factors, in contrast, are reflected in whole asset class markets. While value generally beats growth over the long run, the entire market comprises value *and* growth stocks. In order for a value premium to exist, some investors must be comfortable holding the opposite side of value with lower returns. Put another way, for every value stock there must be a growth stock, and for every value investor there must also be a growth investor. Style factors reflect the relative difference between the observable properties of assets—low or high prices relative to fundamentals for value versus growth, for example—and the style premiums reflect the relative risk of these assets. But style factor premiums arise due to structural impediments or behavioral biases. Let's examine these in the context of value and low-volatility factors.

VALUE: RISK PREMIUM OR BEHAVIORAL BIAS

The risk story behind the value premium is that value firms are riskier because they can't easily change their business practices. Many traditional value firms are old-fashioned service or manufacturing firms. They own specialized equipment that is not easily convertible for other purposes. When the economy slows, these firms not only see lower revenues and profit margins from their shrinking sales, but they are also stuck with unproductive capital stock that cannot be sold because these firms cannot reposition that fixed capital to produce other things. Because value firms are fundamentally riskier than more flexible growth firms,[5] investors may earn a premium for owning them.

The value premium can also be explained by behavioral biases of the average investor: Many investors mistake past performance for future prospects. Investors often gravitate to high-flying companies' stocks with past high-growth rates and naively assume that these past growth rates will extend into the future—and stock prices reflect these over-optimistic growth assumptions. But these growth rates often fall short, and prices eventually decline, leaving traditional value firms to outperform over the long run.

LOW VOLATILITY: STRUCTURAL IMPEDIMENT OR BEHAVIORAL BIAS

The low-volatility risk premium seeks to take advantage of the fact that stocks with low volatilities often have higher risk-adjusted returns than their high-volatility counterparts. The higher risk–return trade-off of low-volatility stocks comes through these stocks having lower risk with no apparent reduction in the average return and historically even higher returns than high-volatility stocks.[6]

The phenomenon can be explained through market structure constraints. Institutional investors like pension funds and endowments have high total return targets but often have limits on how much they can borrow. Therefore, their preferred option would be to take an optimal risky portfolio and then leverage it, and the leverage enables them to put more money to work just as it allows an individual to buy a bigger house. Without

[5]BlackRock, "Factors: What Are They, Why They've Worked, Ways to Get Started" (2016).
[6]Published research showing the historical outperformance of minimum volatility strategies

leverage, they have to choose riskier stocks in the search for higher expected returns. This behavior can bid up the prices of high-volatility and high-beta stocks and push down their expected returns. As a result, unloved lower-risk stocks may be priced at lower levels despite their higher expected returns.

The structural impediment on borrowing is complemented by a behavioral bias to seek higher returns. Investors hungry for profit may buy risky, lottery-ticket-like stocks in the hopes of hitting the jackpot with the next big idea. When an outcome is possible but not probable, behavioral bias pushes us to perceive that the probability of winning is high—even if the odds are stacked against us. Like the leverage constraints, the lottery effect may leave lower risk stocks underpriced.

COMBINING FACTORS

The economic sources behind the individual factor returns imply that the factors are cyclical—just as plain-vanilla equity and bond classes are cyclical. But, they are cyclical at different times. Value tends to perform well early in an economic cycle; its worst performance tends to be at the peak of the cycle when most assets become over-valued or in the troughs when value firms cannot pivot to producing new things. Low-volatility strategies shine, by definition, when the aggregate market is turbulent. Momentum losses come suddenly when there are sharp changes in sentiment. Combining multiple factors rather than just one single investment style can potentially lead to greater diversification benefits over time.

WHAT'S NEW?

All of these factor premiums—macro and style factors—have been known for decades. We are well positioned to take advantage of these risk premiums in global markets, utilizing large datasets and efficient execution. The potential benefits of factor investing—creating more robust portfolios, better risk management, and finding more diversified sources of return—certainly explain why many institutions have embraced factor investing since the financial crisis, but these benefits were well known before this time.

So what's new today?

Done at its best, factor investing has transformed the traditional management of institutional portfolios and become a *management philosophy*: an organizing principle that is up to the task of meeting the complex demands faced by large asset owners.

FACTOR INVESTING IS SIMPLIFYING BUT NOT SIMPLISTIC

Large funds have complicated portfolios: Plain-vanilla, long-only equities and bonds have given way to structured credit, repo, private equity, infrastructure, and long–short alpha strategies. Especially for stakeholders who are not investment professionals, factor investing translates what can often be unintelligible into intuitive factor exposures: macro or style factors. The portfolios can be complex, but the important drivers are more easily explained. As a side benefit, factor investing exposes overlapping risks that could be lurking in investors' portfolios.

FACTOR INVESTING IS FLEXIBLE

A factor-based framework may give management greater flexibility in their investment choices. Just as we can obtain protein in milk, a steak dinner, or a protein shake, factor investing allows chief investment officers (CIOs) to express factors across the full spectrum of available opportunities, ranging from low-cost index strategies to expensive and illiquid alternatives. CIOs can harvest, say, duration in index fixed income, smart beta fixed income, unconstrained active fixed-income managers, and even in illiquid infrastructure funds. Investors can choose where to access these rewarded factors based on their preferences for liquidity, costs, and transparency.

FACTOR INVESTING IS FOR THE TOTAL ENTERPRISE

Today's CIOs don't have the luxury of just investing. They must also consider the needs of beneficiaries, communicate effectively with board members and participants, and satisfy the demands of sponsoring entities. Factors can help bridge these demands. For large asset owners, enterprise risk is as important today as investment risk. Factor investing helps them to mitigate agency risk by decomposing a manager's funds into return drivers. A real estate fund has factor exposures to equity and debt. Knowing the debt exposure allows owners to monitor overall leverage across their portfolios.

FACTOR INVESTING DRIVES COLLABORATION

At many large institutions, investment staff covering private assets communicate poorly with their public market counterparts. In extreme cases, a division focusing only on one asset class runs its own fiefdom, without regard to the overall objectives of the fund. In these circumstances, factor investing can provide a common thread running throughout the organization. It can enable different asset class managers—internal and external, public and private markets, beta and alpha-seeking—to work together by providing a common language regardless of asset class or investment style.

CONCLUSION

The full power of factor investing, it turns out, is more than just investing in factors. At the leading institutions embracing factor investing for their total portfolios, it has become a total management philosophy and a culture—a powerful and empowering way of running an entire asset management institution.

2. Risk Factor Investing: The Case for Exotic Beta

Mark Carhart, CFA
Chief Investment Officer, Kepos Capital

Institutional investors have undertaken significant efforts to better manage and balance risk. While progress has been made, much work still lies ahead. Most portfolios remain severely imbalanced, with the typical portfolio still dominated by equity and equity-like risks. This remains true even after the broad-based reallocation of capital to other assets and alternatives.

Ten years ago, well before the financial crisis, we began discussing exotic betas, a concept that is sometimes referred to as "alternative risk premiums," "risk-factor investing," or "smart betas." We define exotic betas as exposures to risk factors that are both uncorrelated with global equity markets and have positive expected returns. We describe them as existing on a continuum between alpha and the widely known equity market beta. **Figure 2.1** shows this continuum. Like alpha, they are a source of uncorrelated returns to most portfolios, but unlike alpha, they are not opportunities captured by unique active management skills. Exotic betas are compensated risk factors—either from risk transfers or from behavioral effects—for which investors earn excess returns. They are transparent and relatively well known. What differentiates them is simply the source of the return.

FIGURE 2.1. ALTERNATIVE RISK FACTORS ON THE CONTINUUM BETWEEN ALPHA AND EQUITY MARKET BETA

DEFINING THE FACTORS

As there is no theory that specifically defines what the risk factors are, where they can be found, or how they can be best accessed, we propose that the first steps in this process should be to create a taxonomy and a set of criteria for identifying and categorizing factors. Most importantly, the process should be designed to identify factors that can be expected to persist in the future. This is distinctly different from an approach that begins with scouring the data for factors that have worked well in the past. Such a process tends to identify factors that are over-fit and not robust. In other words, an approach that begins with finding what worked best in the past is likely to find factors that will disappoint in the future.

In this discussion, we focus on macro risk factors (i.e., not including stock-specific factors) and propose the following basic taxonomy. You may note that other risk premium themes are not included. For example, liquidity premiums are not included as we believe they can be accessed more effectively in private assets. Similarly, a "defensive" theme, which typically includes Treasury Inflation-Protected Securities and tail-hedging strategies, is not included because we want to take on a diversified set of risks that yield compensation; such strategies produce the opposite—one gives up return to reduce risk. Lastly, we exclude "hedge fund–oriented" factors, such as convertible arbitrage and merger arbitrage, because our goal is to deliver exposure to macro factors, not to replicate an active strategy. In the case of merger arbitrage, for example, the returns are similar to those obtained from selling uncovered index put options. We look for the underlying risk factors that explain such strategies. **Figure 2.2** illustrates how we categorize risk premium types.

FIGURE 2.2. RISK PREMIUM AND ASSET CLASS CATEGORIES

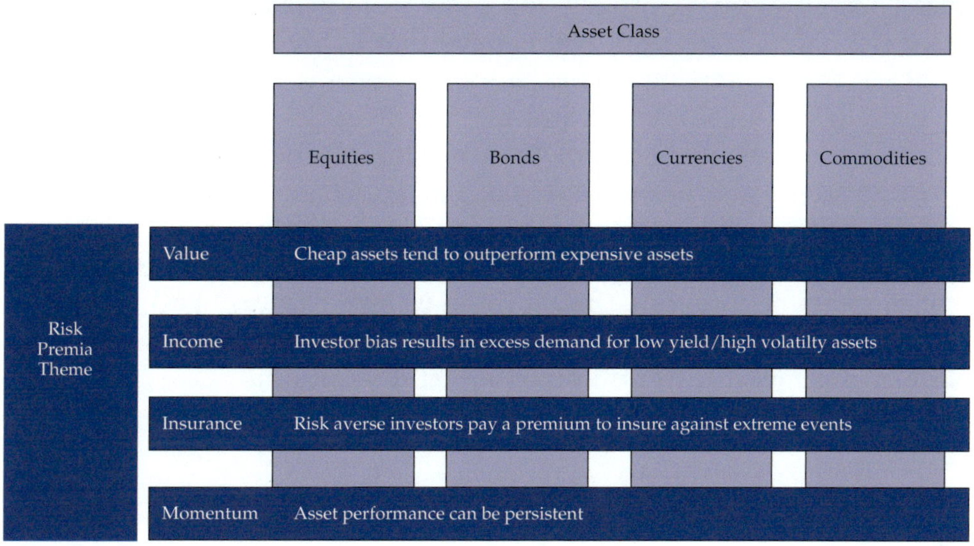

We also propose selection criterion that combines intuition with rigorous robustness testing. While intuition is important, stories alone do not guarantee that a factor that has worked in the past will work in the future. One needs to balance economic intuition with empirical robustness. We try to maximize robustness by requiring that each factor meet a set of stringent criteria:

1. Economic intuition (must be driven by risk transfer or persistent behavioral effect)
2. Demonstrated historical premium in excess of global equity risk premium
3. Sufficient liquidity and capacity for broad institutional access
4. Must be empirically robust:

a. Logic must be testable on other markets, asset classes, and time periods

b. Must hold up when specific time periods and/or markets are excluded ("jack-knifing")

c. Must be insensitive to factor definition so that it can be "ensembled" by averaging across many factor specifications

BUILDING A PORTFOLIO OF FACTORS

The primary benefit of this approach will come from a balanced exposure to a diversified set of risk factors. As such, we believe that applying equal risk to individual factors is a reasonable starting point. However, there is value to strategically tilting across factors. Relative confidence and historical results, as well as forecasted correlations, can be reasonable bases for tactical tilts. Moreover, slow-moving, modest, dynamic reallocations may be warranted due to structural changes, broad changes in market risk appetite, and the valuation of individual risk factors. In this presentation, we propose a Bayesian risk-budgeting process, illustrated in **Figure 2.3**, that combines a set of strategic forecasts (based on long-term "priors" and historical performance) with dynamic forecasts that incorporate factor valuation, factor momentum, and "spillover," our measure of potential market disruption.

FIGURE 2.3. BAYESIAN RISK-BUDGETING PROCESS

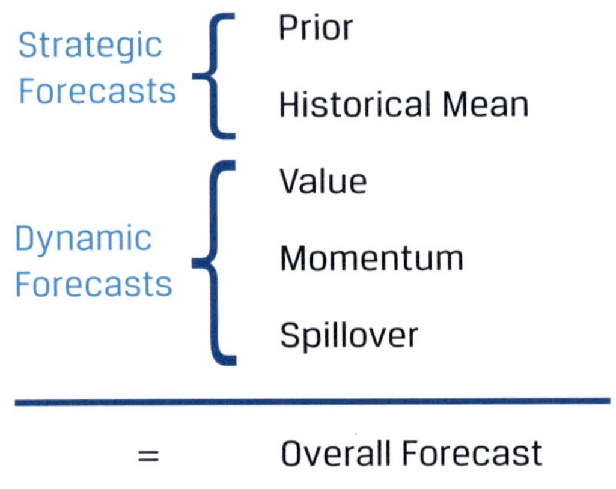

HISTORICAL PERFORMANCE

Figure 2.4 shows the results of a historical backtest of the strategy discussed in the presentation. It shows the returns of the four risk premium themes, the overall exotic beta portfolio, and the returns of global equities, all standardized to the same volatility. It shows that exotic betas can offer attractive long-term returns, more consistent performance than traditional asset classes, and low correlation to the global equity markets. Some of these factors are already embedded in the typical institutional portfolio; more purposeful management of these exposures can lead to better balance and diversification. In addition, while an exotic beta portfolio is attractive as a standalone absolute return strategy, its application is even more compelling in the context of the broader investment portfolio. Its high Sharpe ratio and low correlation to global equities lead to a reduction in the risk concentration in equities, an enhancement of returns, and a reduction of overall portfolio risk.

Figure 2.4 shows historic performance above one-month US T-bills of backtested risk premiums that include real-world trading constraints, estimated *t*-costs, and a hedge to the MSCI ACWI, from January 1990 to December 2014.

FIGURE 2.4. RISK FACTOR THEMES AND TOTAL FACTOR PORTFOLIO

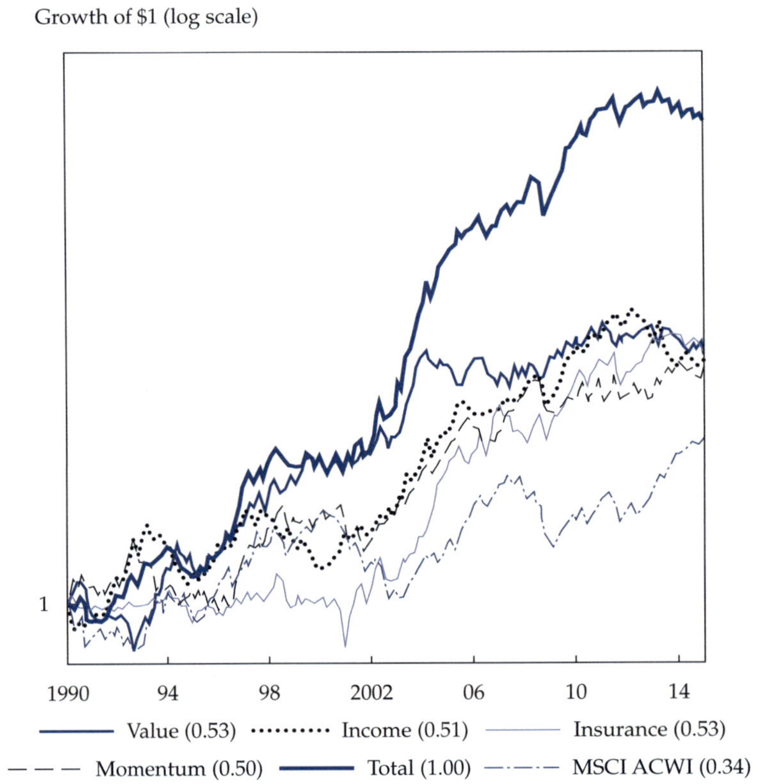

Prospective investors should exercise caution in using or relying on any hypothetical or backtested results as being indicative of future performance. THESE RESULTS ARE BASED ON SIMULATED OR HYPOTHETICAL PERFORMANCE RESULTS THAT HAVE CERTAIN INHERENT LIMITATIONS. UNLIKE THE RESULTS SHOWN IN AN ACTUAL PERFORMANCE RECORD, THESE RESULTS DO NOT REPRESENT ACTUAL TRADING. ALSO, BECAUSE THE TRADES HAVE NOT ACTUALLY BEEN EXECUTED, THE RESULTS MAY HAVE UNDER- OR OVER-COMPENSATED FOR THE IMPACT, IF ANY, OF CERTAIN MARKET FACTORS, SUCH AS LACK OF LIQUIDITY. SIMULATED OR HYPOTHETICAL TRADING PROGRAMS IN GENERAL ARE ALSO SUBJECT TO THE FACT THAT THEY ARE DESIGNED WITH THE BENEFIT OF HINDSIGHT. NO REPRESENTATION IS BEING MADE THAT ANY ACCOUNT WILL OR IS LIKELY TO ACHIEVE PROFITS OR LOSSES SIMILAR TO THESE BEING SHOWN. MSCI ACWI is an index designed to measure the broad equity market performance of developed and emerging markets. (Please see important backtest disclosures on the next page.)

PAST PERFORMANCE IS NOT AN INDICATOR OR GUARANTEE OF FUTURE RESULTS. THERE IS NO GUARANTEE THAT THE FUND WILL ACHIEVE COMPARABLE RESULTS TO THOSE SET FORTH IN THIS DOCUMENT OR THAT IT WILL ACHIEVE ITS INVESTMENT OBJECTIVES IN THE FUTURE.

The information in this Presentation is believed accurate and is given only as of the date set forth on the cover and Kepos undertakes no obligation to update such information. This Presentation is provided for discussion purposes only, is only a summary of certain information, is not complete, does not contain certain material information about the Fund, including important conflicts disclosures and risk factors, and is subject to change without notice.

This Presentation does not constitute an offer to sell or a solicitation of an offer to purchase any security of any investible product. Any such offer or solicitation shall only be made pursuant to—and subject to the terms and conditions contained in—a confidential private placement memorandum of such investible product (and an accompanying subscription agreement), which qualifies in its entirety the information set forth herein, which should be read carefully prior to an investment in such investible product, and which contains additional information about the investment objectives, terms and conditions, tax information and risk disclosures of or relating to such investible product.

An investment in any investible product is not suitable for all investors. Investors must meet certain eligibility requirements and have the financial ability, sophistication, experience, and willingness to bear the risks of an investment in such investible product for an extended period of time. An investment in such investible product would be speculative and entails a high degree of risk; no assurance can be given that such investible product's investment objective will be achieved or that investors will receive a return of their capital. Investment losses may occur. Nothing herein is intended to imply that any investible product's investment methodology may be considered "conservative," "safe," "risk free," or "risk averse."

Certain of the information contained in this Presentation represents or is based upon forward-looking statements, which can be identified by the use of forward-looking terminology such as "may", "will", "should", "expect", "anticipate", "target", "project", "estimate", "intend", "continue" or "believe" or the negatives thereof or other variations thereon or comparable terminology. Due to various risks and uncertainties, actual events or results or the actual performance of the Fund may differ materially from those reflected or contemplated in such forward-looking statements. The information contained herein represents management's current expectation of how the Fund will continue to be operated in the near term; however, management's plans and policies in this respect may change in the future. In particular, (i) policies and approaches to portfolio monitoring, risk management, and asset allocation may change in the future without notice and (ii) economic, market and other conditions could cause the Fund to deviate from stated investment objectives and guidelines.

This document is confidential, is intended only for the person to whom it has been provided and under no circumstance may a copy be shown, copied, transmitted, or otherwise given to any person other than the authorized recipient without the prior written consent of Kepos. Notwithstanding anything to the contrary herein, each recipient of this summary may disclose to any and all persons, without limitation of any kind, the tax treatment and tax structure of: (i) the Fund and (ii) any of its transactions, and all materials of any kind (including opinions or other tax analyses) relating to such tax treatment and tax structure. The distribution of the information contained herein in certain jurisdictions may be restricted, and, accordingly, it is the responsibility of any prospective investor to satisfy itself as to compliance with relevant laws and regulations.

References to indices, benchmarks or other measures of relative market performance over a specified period of time are provided for your information only and do not imply that the actual Fund portfolio will achieve similar results. The index composition does not reflect the manner in which a portfolio is constructed; unlike these indices and benchmarks, the Fund's portfolio may contain options (including covered and uncovered puts and calls) and other derivative securities, futures and other commodity interests and currencies, and may include short sales of securities, margin trading, securities of smaller capitalization companies and types of securities that are different than those reflected in these indices and benchmarks, and is not as diversified as these indices and benchmarks. While an adviser seeks to design a portfolio which reflects appropriate risk and return features, portfolio characteristics may deviate from those of the benchmark. Indices are unmanaged and investors cannot invest directly in most indices. The figures for the indices may reflect the reinvestment of dividends but do not reflect the deduction of any fees or expenses which would reduce returns.

To the extent simulations, hypothetical returns and/or backtests were used to prepare this presentation:

THESE RESULTS ARE BASED ON SIMULATED OR HYPOTHETICAL PERFORMANCE RESULTS THAT HAVE CERTAIN INHERENT LIMITATIONS. UNLIKE THE RESULTS SHOWN IN AN ACTUAL PERFORMANCE RECORD, THESE RESULTS DO NOT REPRESENT ACTUAL TRADING. ALSO, BECAUSE THE TRADES HAVE NOT ACTUALLY BEEN EXECUTED, THE RESULTS MAY HAVE UNDER- OR OVER-COMPENSATED FOR THE IMPACT, IF ANY, OF CERTAIN MARKET FACTORS, SUCH AS LACK OF LIQUIDITY. SIMULATED OR HYPOTHETICAL TRADING PROGRAMS IN GENERAL ARE ALSO SUBJECT TO THE FACT THAT THEY ARE DESIGNED WITH THE BENEFIT OF HINDSIGHT. NO REPRESENTATION IS BEING MADE THAT ANY ACCOUNT WILL OR IS LIKELY TO ACHIEVE PROFITS OR LOSSES SIMILAR TO THESE BEING SHOWN.

HOW THE SIMULATIONS WERE COMPILED

- *Multiple Concurrent Models.* For the exotic beta strategy, we employ 33 trading models. The models were used to construct the individual exotic betas. Further, a model was employed that, based on systematic criteria, varied the amount of risk allocated to each exotic beta throughout the simulation. We group the individual exotic betas into four themes: value, income, insurance, and momentum.

- *Hypothetical Returns.* The results presented were achieved by retroactively applying the trading models to market data for various time periods, depending on a discretionary decision by us as to the reliability of the market data for use in backtesting for each strategy. The inception dates for each strategy may differ based on availability of data. For the full sample results: January 1990 to December 2014 is the date for value; January 1990 to December 2014 is the date for income; February 1990 to December 2014 is the date for insurance; and January 1990 to December 2014 is the date for momentum.

- *Calculation of Returns.* Returns are based on excess return above the respective financing rate that would have been experienced by the applicable tradable instrument utilized, inclusive of mark-to-market gains and losses and all cash flows (including cash flows that were related to dividends or other distributions) that would have been realized. The simulated performance is presented gross of any management and incentive fees.

- *Transaction Costs Estimate.* Transaction costs are imputed in all values presented and are calculated through the application of an overall algorithm for each strategy created using historical data for the entire period surveyed that computes—for each given hypothetical transaction—a bid–ask spread and expected market impact for such transactions, which may not equal the actual spread and market impact that would have applied in any given case.

- *Sizing Individual Exotic Betas to Form the Exotic Beta Strategy.* The amount of risk allocated to individual exotic betas has varied throughout the simulation. The target risk allocated to each exotic beta was determined frequently (e.g., monthly) during the time span of the applicable simulation using only backward-looking information from a variety of sources, including strategy backtests, prior beliefs, and expected diversification benefits.

- *Other Constraints.* The simulated underlying portfolios may also include a number of additional constraints. These were imposed at the discretion of Kepos personnel and are meant to represent (but may not accurately forecast) what may happen in actual trading (e.g., volume limitations in certain securities). For each portfolio/strategy that you consider to be material or of interest, we can provide additional information on any such constraints.

- *Humbled Returns* are total discounted backtested returns estimated by applying a constant haircut to the total returns of the original undiscounted backtested returns. This haircut is attributed to the underlying asset classes/strategies in proportion to their average contribution to the original undiscounted backtest. The haircut used in this simulation corresponds to a 65% discount on the average return of the original backtest.

3. The Perils of Forecasting

Craig Bodenstab, CFA
Orbis Investment Advisory (Canada) Limited

Forming a view about the future is an essential part of everyday life, and many aspects of day-to-day life are relatively easy to predict with a high degree of accuracy. Unfortunately for investors, forming a view about the future of financial markets, or asset prices more specifically, is not as easy as predicting what time the sun will rise each day or how much a cup of coffee will cost. Not surprisingly, our industry has a horrendous track record trying to predict the future. However, in spite of this, investment managers continue to have strong incentives to forecast and to do so precisely and confidently. As luck would have it, often even good forecasts don't lead to better investment results.

Investors should think twice about the weight they place on forecasts and should instead focus on what they can control: the price they pay for assets.

FORECASTING IN EVERYDAY LIFE VS. FINANCIAL MARKETS

Nearly everything we do in life relies on expectations about the future, and this is fine because many things are relatively easy to predict. Take, for example, chemistry. Regardless of the chemist's mood, what her peers think, or whether the Federal Reserve raises interest rates, she knows that water is two parts hydrogen and one part oxygen. She can count on this relationship to hold every time!

Unfortunately, when it comes to investing, we cannot (to nearly the same degree) count on past relationships to always hold. Physics has Newton's laws of motion; investing has "past performance is not an indicator of future results." What drives this difference?

In science and similar disciplines, knowledge is generally cumulative, building on a foundation of laws and relationships. In the financial world, knowledge is adaptive, in the sense that the views and actions of each participant—a function of their own experiences—affect the views and actions of others. As John Maynard Keynes put it, investors are like judges in a beauty contest where the goal is to pick not the most beautiful contestant but the contestant who is picked by the most other judges. The result is a dizzying degree of interdependence as each judge tries to guess what other judges will think other judges will do. This keeps markets in a constant state of reflexive flux, making it difficult to forecast with any degree of precision.

If making predictions within an adaptive system is so difficult, why is our industry still so committed to trying to precisely predict the future?

THE APPEAL OF FORECASTING

Investors try to maximize returns while minimizing risks—and uncertainty is a major risk. From an investment manager's perspective, even the slightest possibility of being right is generally better than the alternative of telling your clients, "I don't know."

Clients often ask where the Canadian dollar or the fed funds rate or the S&P 500 Index will be next year. The honest answer is that we don't know, but clients have views on these things as well, and the "I don't know" response makes them question why they hired a manager who seems to know much less than they do. It follows that as long as asset managers' livelihoods depend on their clients' confidence in their abilities, "I don't know" is generally not good for business. Given this, investment managers have a strong incentive to forecast—and to do so precisely and confidently.

But too often the precision is false and the confidence misplaced. Understand that for every financial event being forecasted, there are so many different (and conflicting) forecasts that some will end up looking prophetic, and our industry will generally celebrate this success as skill. For clients and money managers alike, when it comes to trying to assess skill, it is imperative to challenge track records by looking at all forecasts made by an individual—not just their latest victory.

A LOOK AT OUR INDUSTRY'S TRACK RECORD

To test the skill of forecasters, we looked at several well-known series and compared one-year forecasts made in January 1990 by "professional" forecasters with actual results. We quantified this comparison by calculating the R^2, or coefficient of determination. A value of 100% means that the variation in one factor "explains" all of the variation in the other factor, while a value of zero means that the variation in one factor explains none of the other's variation.

Table 3.1 shows the R^2 of each series on a unlagged and lagged basis (why we have done this will become clearer in a moment). At first glance, column 1 seems to show that the forecast series aligned quite well with the actual results. Unfortunately, column 1 compares one-year forward estimates with the actual data on the date the estimates were made, not the date the estimates were for. In other words, the one-year forward estimates made in January 1990 need to be compared with the actual results in January 1991, not January 1990.

TABLE 3.1. EXPLANATORY POWER OF ONE-YEAR FORECASTS (UNLAGGED VS. LAGGED)

	1	2
Series	R^2 (unlagged)	R^2 (lagged)
US inflation	87%	71%
US 10-year bond yields	90	65
S&P 500 Index earnings	99	94
WTI crude oil spot price	77	5
CSI 300 Index price	81	13

Source: Bloomberg and Datastream.

To properly assess the quality of these predictions, then, we need to lag the forecast series to allow an apples-to-apples (or forecasted 1991 to actual 1991) comparison with the actual series. This is what is shown in column 2. In every series tested, the forecasts had more "explanatory power" for what was happening at the time the forecast was made than the actual future results. In decision making, this is a cognitive bias referred to as anchoring, which can be particularly dangerous if left unchecked.

As a group, investors appear to be poor forecasters. But what if you were the exception and *could* forecast accurately—would that lead to better investment results?

EVEN ACCURATE FORECASTS MAY NOT ALWAYS BE HELPFUL

Consider GDP growth, one of the most closely followed measures in our industry. Does accurately forecasting GDP growth give you an edge in picking stocks? Surprisingly not—looking at 183 10-year investment periods in 83 countries, the correlation between real GDP growth per capita and real equity returns is an insignificant 0.12.[7] How can this be?

Part of the reason is the relationship between expectations and prices. If investors observe high growth in a particular country and as a result become enthusiastic about shares in that market, that enthusiasm invariably pushes share prices up, thereby reducing subsequent shareholder returns even if companies deliver solid growth.

Even more targeted forecasting may not be especially valuable either. Imagine going back to 1975 armed with perfect knowledge about how the world would look today. You would know that the IT and computer industry has grown significantly faster than even the most optimistic expectations of 40 years ago and that smoking has gone from ubiquitous to ubiquitously scorned. Both of these outcomes were (generally) not foreseen in the 1970s. Armed with this perfect knowledge, you might look to buy shares in the most successful technology companies while avoiding or shorting the leading tobacco companies. **Table 3.2** shows how this strategy would have worked out.

TABLE 3.2. CUMULATIVE RETURNS OF TECHNOLOGY AND TOBACCO LEADERS (1975–2015)

Stock	Cumulative Return
Digital Equipment (industry #2 in 1975)	7 times[a]
IBM (#1)	43 times
Philip Morris (#1)	1,400 times
British American Tobacco (#2)	4,000 times

[a]Return up to Digital Equipment's 1998 acquisition by Compaq.

Source: Datastream.

While the technology industry experienced rapid growth, this growth attracted massive competition and innovation and much of the profits that remained accrued to new entrants rather than to the incumbents of 1975. On the other hand, tobacco has seen falling volumes in the developed world, increased taxes, massive lawsuits, and a ban on advertising. No investor in their right mind would have gone into this business. But there is one critical difference between these two industries—the taxes, lawsuits, and regulations of the tobacco industry have discouraged new entrants (competition),

[7]Elroy Dimson, Paul Marsh, and Mike Staunton, *Global Investment Returns Yearbook 2010* (Credit Suisse Research Institute, 2010) and Elroy Dimson, Paul Marsh, and Mike Staunton, *Triumph of the Optimists* (Princeton, NJ: Princeton University Press, 2002).

which has allowed the remaining companies to pass on these extra costs in the form of higher prices to their customers while leaving attractive returns in the form of dividends and earnings growth for shareholders.

So the bad news is that not only is making accurate forecasts in financial markets very difficult, but even if you get it right, it may not always help. The good news is that what really matters in generating respectable long-term returns is something well within your control—the price you pay for assets.

FOCUS ON WHAT YOU CAN CONTROL

There is a strong correlation between starting valuations, which is a function of the price you pay, and subsequent equity returns. For investment practitioners aiming to generate respectable long-term returns, the most important thing is the price you pay for assets, and this is entirely within your control. By focusing on prices rather than predictions, investors can get a much better sense for what expectations are already priced into a particular security. The job of an analyst, then, is to evaluate whether these expectations are reasonable or not.

To be clear, we are not suggesting that investors stick their heads in the sand and stop thinking about the future. We are simply cautioning investors from placing too much weight on forecasts. History shows that as an industry, we are horrible forecasters and that even when we can forecast accurately this does not guarantee a better investment decision. Spending too much time and effort forecasting may be the reason that some 75% of professionally managed funds underperform the S&P 500![8]

Focus instead on what you can control and what matters most: the price you pay for assets.

[8]Charles Ellis, *Winning the Loser's Game* (New York: McGraw-Hill, 2002).

4. Using Good Judgment for Financial Analysis

Philip E. Tetlock
University of Pennsylvania and Good Judgment Inc.

Warren Hatch, CFA
Good Judgment Inc.

Many of the tools of the Superforecaster trade will be familiar to financial analysts, particularly members of CFA Institute: be open minded, update your assessments regularly, be aware of innate biases and how to deal with them, and embrace flexibility. Less familiar is how the Superforecasters honed their skills on a forecasting platform, offering a way for financial analysts to refine their skills and for financial institutions to enhance how they aggregate analyst research.

GOOD JUDGMENT

The Superforecasters were the top-performing 2% of volunteer forecasters at the Good Judgment Project, part of a four-year tournament sponsored by the US government's Intelligence Advanced Research Projects Activity (IARPA). After the first year, not only did the Good Judgment Project exceed the initial goals of the tournament but also the improvement in forecast accuracy hit the target set for the fourth year of the competition (Tetlock and Gardner 2015). After the second year, IARPA ended the formal tournament and consolidated its resources solely on the processes being developed by Good Judgment. At the conclusion of the program in June 2015, Steve Rieber, the program manager at IARPA, summarized the results as "the largest improvement in judgmental forecasting accuracy observed in the literature" (Rieber 2015).

Here are three of the key findings from the Good Judgment Project that can be helpful for financial professionals: small improvements in forecast accuracy add up, keeping score is essential to get the feedback that improves accuracy, and forecasting is a skill that can be best cultivated in dedicated forecasting tournaments.

SMALL IMPROVEMENTS ADD UP

In a blurry world, Good Judgment's best methods improve foresight using tools developed and refined through the course of the four-year study. Initial conditions matter, and selecting individuals with the right mix of traits alone can boost forecast accuracy by up to 40%. Spotting and cultivating talented forecasters takes time but is worth the effort. Next, training in probabilities and bias awareness can boost accuracy by another 10%. Forecasting on teams facilitates error checking and, done properly, avoids the pitfalls of groupthink to provide another 10% boost. Finally, the careful use of algorithms to overweight shrewd forecasters and extremize aggregated forecasts to compensate for individual conservatism can boost accuracy by up to 25%.

Good Judgment's methods help analysts and portfolio managers improve their focus on what can happen in the future. For example, there is much value to be had from taking an initial forecast of, say, a coin flip with 50/50 odds and arriving at a more accurate probability estimate that is slightly higher or lower. In such cases, consistently accurate forecasts of 55% for a long position (or 45% for a short position) can be a compelling proposition.

Some of these tools can be applied in nearly any financial institution, such as for personnel selection and de-bias training. Other tools, such as the use of team-based forecasting, may be more challenging to implement but the payoffs can boost the bottom line.

KEEPING SCORE IS KEY

Regular feedback on results allows learning to occur from the successes just as much the failures. The specific metric Good Judgment selected to track forecasting performance is the Brier Score, which provides a cumulative grade that compares daily forecasts against the eventual outcome of a question. On this scale, a score of zero means you had perfect insight and assigned a 100% probability from day one to an event that did occur (or conversely, 0% to something that did not occur). A score of 2 means you got everything completely wrong. And 0.5 is consistent with random guessing along with the proverbial dart-throwing chimp. An important feature of this scoring system is that the cost of being "wrong" is twice the reward for being "right," which incentivizes forecasters to report their true forecasts and avoid extreme forecasts unless they have high conviction.

With regular and robust feedback, forecasters learn to improve their calibration. Say they forecast a series of five questions with an 80% probability of occurring. If four of those forecasts subsequently happen and the fifth does not, then those forecasters are well calibrated and 80% is a good estimate of probability. It can take time and a lot of practice to achieve that level of calibration. For many people, things became particularly tricky in the tails of the bell curve, where forecasts of 95% end up happening far less frequently and forecasts of 5% happen more often. Given how Brier Scores work, it is a bruising experience to be scored for over-confidence and under-confidence alike. Improved calibration is the reward for the hardy souls who persist and learn.

In short, recognizing more shades of gray improves accuracy in the middle of the bell curve while better calibration improves accuracy in the tails.

FORECASTING TOURNAMENTS ARE THE BEST WAY TO LEARN

Superforecasters are finely calibrated throughout the bell curve and helped by well-targeted training, extensive experience with a lot of feedback, and the right environment to put it all together. As Good Judgment found, the best environment is in a forecasting tournament. For individuals, outside distractions are kept to a minimum, feedback is direct, and they can benefit from team interaction within a culture of collaborative competition. Tournaments create a level playing field to determine who knows what for the question at hand, which can help organizations improve their existing decision-making processes.

In the shifting competitive landscape of the financial industry, forecasting tournaments represent a disruptive technology that can rejuvenate organizations with stale status quo hierarchies and give an edge to forward-looking firms.

REFERENCES

Reiber, Steve. 2015. "CREATE Proposers' Day, IARPA." (30 June).

Tetlock, Philip E., and Dan Gardner. 2015. *Superforecasting: The Art and Science of Prediction.* New York: Crown.

5. Forecasting Asset Returns in Realistic Environments

David E. Rapach
Saint Louis University

Forecasting asset returns is an intellectually fascinating endeavor with important implications. From the standpoint of finance practitioners, improved asset return forecasts offer the opportunity to substantially improve investment performance. From an academic standpoint, understanding asset return predictability is crucial to the development of theoretical asset pricing models that better explain real-world phenomena.

However, forecasting asset returns can also be frustrating. Asset returns inherently contain a large unpredictable component, so that even the best models explain only a relatively small part of return fluctuations. Indeed, if an asset return forecasting model sounds too good to be true, it surely is. Nevertheless, a little goes a long way: Even a seemingly small degree of return predictability in a statistical sense can generate significant performance gains for investors.

Another frustrating aspect of asset return forecasting is that the widespread adoption of a successful model can eliminate its forecasting ability, so that the very success of a model can lead to its ultimate undoing. However, to the extent that a forecasting model captures asset return predictability that stems from time-varying systematic risk premiums and/or "pockets" of market inefficiencies due to limits to arbitrage, its forecasting ability should continue going forward. In support of this notion, a sizable body of academic research suggests that time-varying risk premiums and limits to arbitrage play key roles in asset pricing.

How can we best forecast asset returns? Using the insightful analogy from *Superforecasting*, the superb new book by Philip Tetlock and Dan Gardner discussed in the previous section, recent research indicates that it is far better to be a *fox* than a *hedgehog*. A hedgehog follows a single, narrow strategy to solve all problems—a "one-size-fits-all" approach. In contrast, a fox is versatile and tries a variety of ways to solve a problem—a much more flexible approach.

To state the obvious, we do not know "The Model" of asset returns. Indeed, the actual data-generating process for asset returns is highly complex and constantly evolving, so that forecasters face substantial model *uncertainty* and *instability*. In such an environment, a hedgehog approach is highly inadvisable. While a hedgehog approach—for example, relying solely on a "go-to" predictor variable to forecast the market return—can perform quite well at certain times, it also inevitably experiences extended periods when it performs poorly, precisely because the approach fails to accommodate model uncertainty and instability.

Instead of relying on a single favorite predictor variable, a "foxy" forecasting approach utilizes information from a wide array of potentially relevant predictors, in explicit recognition of model uncertainty and instability. When incorporating information from a plethora of predictors, however, it is crucial to avoid model *overfitting*. The last thing that a forecaster should do is estimate an unrestricted "kitchen sink" model that includes a host of potential predictors as explanatory variables. Although such a model typically produces impressive in-sample fit—indeed, conventional ordinary least-squares estimation maximizes the in-sample fit—it is well known that it usually performs very poorly when it comes to out-of-sample forecasting. Overfitting is a particularly relevant concern for asset return forecasting, as it is all too easy to overreact to noise in the predictor variables.

Fortunately, recent research points to promising strategies for improving asset return forecasts in realistic environments with substantial model uncertainty and instability. Specifically, recent research highlights *forecast combination* and *diffusion indices* as beneficial approaches for incorporating information from many predictors while avoiding overfitting. Forecast combination takes a simple average of the forecasts generated by a large number of underlying models, each of which is based on an individual predictor. Rapach, Strauss, and Zhou (2010) show that forecast combination avoids overfitting by effectively shrinking parameter estimates, and they find that this approach significantly improves forecasts of the US equity risk premium.

The diffusion index approach avoids overfitting by extracting the first few principal components from the entire set of potential predictors, with the principal components subsequently serving as explanatory variables in the forecasting model. Principal components filter out much of the noise from the individual predictors to provide a more reliable signal. Ludvigson and Ng (2007) and Neely, Rapach, Tu, and Zhou (2014) show that, like forecast combination, the diffusion index approach generates improved US equity risk premium forecasts.

Recent studies indicate that the forecast combination and diffusion index strategies significantly enhance investment performance. For example, in an application involving 25 size-/value-sorted stock portfolios, Kong, Rapach, Strauss, and Zhou (2011) find that combination forecasts of returns for the 25 portfolios constitute valuable inputs for allocating across the portfolios on a monthly basis. In addition, Almadi, Rapach, and Suri (2014) show that diffusion index forecasts of US bill, bond, and stock returns provide valuable guidance for dynamic asset allocation for an investor who "tilts" away from strategic benchmark portfolio weights.

In sum, recent research develops foxy strategies for forecasting asset returns in realistic environments with substantial model uncertainty and instability; see Rapach and Zhou (2013) for an extensive survey of this literature. Although the predictable component in asset returns is necessarily small, recent research indicates that carefully conceived forecasting approaches deliver improved asset return forecasts that warrant the attention of investors.

REFERENCES

Almadi, H., D.E. Rapach, and A. Suri. 2014. "Return Predictability and Dynamic Asset Allocation: How Often Should Investors Rebalance?" *Journal of Portfolio Management*, vol. 40, no. 4: 16–27.

Kong, A., D.E. Rapach, J.K. Strauss, and G. Zhou. 2011. "Predicting Market Components Out of Sample: Asset Allocation Implications." *Journal of Portfolio Management*, vol. 37, no. 4: 29–41.

Ludvigson, S.C., and S. Ng. 2007. "The Empirical Risk–Return Relation: A Factor Analysis Approach." *Journal of Financial Economics*, vol. 83, no. 1: 171–222.

Neely, C.J., D.E. Rapach, J. Tu, and G. Zhou. 2014. "Forecasting the Equity Risk Premium: The Role of Technical Indicators." *Management Science*, vol. 60, no. 7: 1772–1791.

Rapach, D.E., and G. Zhou. 2013. "Forecasting Stock Returns." In *Handbook of Economic Forecasting*, vol. 2A. Edited by G. Elliott and A. Timmermann. Amsterdam: Elsevier: 328–383.

Rapach, D.E., J.K Strauss, and G. Zhou. 2010. "Out-of-Sample Equity Premium Prediction: Combination Forecasts and Links to the Real Economy." *Review of Financial Studies*, vol. 23, no. 2: 821–862.

Named Endowments

The CFA Institute Research Foundation acknowledges with sincere gratitude the generous contributions of the Named Endowment participants listed below.

Gifts of at least US$100,000 qualify donors for membership in the Named Endowment category, which recognizes in perpetuity the commitment toward unbiased, practitioner-oriented, relevant research that these firms and individuals have expressed through their generous support of the CFA Institute Research Foundation.

Ameritech
Anonymous
Robert D. Arnott
Theodore R. Aronson, CFA
Asahi Mutual Life
Batterymarch Financial Management
Boston Company
Boston Partners Asset Management, L.P.
Gary P. Brinson, CFA
Brinson Partners, Inc.
Capital Group International, Inc.
Concord Capital Management
Dai-Ichi Life Company
Daiwa Securities
Mr. and Mrs. Jeffrey Diermeier
Gifford Fong Associates
Investment Counsel Association of America, Inc.
Jacobs Levy Equity Management
John A. Gunn, CFA
John B. Neff
Jon L. Hagler Foundation
Long-Term Credit Bank of Japan, Ltd.
Lynch, Jones & Ryan, LLC
Meiji Mutual Life Insurance Company
Miller Anderson & Sherrerd, LLP
Nikko Securities Co., Ltd.
Nippon Life Insurance Company of Japan
Nomura Securities Co., Ltd.
Payden & Rygel
Provident National Bank
Frank K. Reilly, CFA
Salomon Brothers
Sassoon Holdings Pte. Ltd.
Scudder Stevens & Clark
Security Analysts Association of Japan
Shaw Data Securities, Inc.
Sit Investment Associates, Inc.
Standish, Ayer & Wood, Inc.
State Farm Insurance Company
Sumitomo Life America, Inc.
T. Rowe Price Associates, Inc.
Templeton Investment Counsel Inc.
Frank Trainer, CFA
Travelers Insurance Co.
USF&G Companies
Yamaichi Securities Co., Ltd.

Senior Research Fellows

Financial Services Analyst Association

For more on upcoming Research Foundation publications and webcasts, please visit www.cfainstitute.org/learning/foundation.

Research Foundation monographs are online at www.cfapubs.org.

Made in the USA
Monee, IL
09 May 2026

49764758R00024